Raised Ranch

poems by

Lauren Singer

Raised Ranch

ISBN: 979-8-9915566-8-2

Cover design by Catherine Weiss

Edited by Catherine Weiss

www.gameoverbooks.com

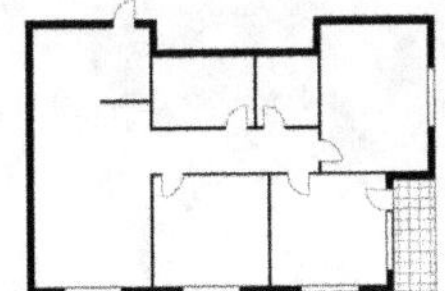

For Ziggy. His Lilacs. His Hawks.
& those who have kept their lights on for him.

Eat-in Kitchen

Nana's Dead

Another day and
Nana's dead.
Rise clumsily from sleep at 5pm
on a Saturday, Nana's dead.
Don't look in the mirror, bad Jew Shiva.
Nana's dead.
Eat chocolate cake to commemorate her life
because she's dead. And tomorrow she will still be dead.
When you have the dream about her body
and how it is clawing at you,
begging to get her out of the bed, out of that place,
remember that she is dead.
That sometimes death is the thing you pray for.

You said, *darling you must pray that I die very soon because I cannot take this pain* but you couldn't tell me what the pain was and maybe it was just of being Alive for 98 years knowing that nothing was ever in your control and the illusion of days passing just becomes a metronome when your body fails you and the sweet late-shift nurse's aide talks on her speaker phone all night and calls you honey and you say *thank you thank you thank you darling* but you want to say fuck you fuck you fuck you and her working legs and her after-work plans and all her sunny optimism all her telling you not to cry and you don't know what you're crying about but it doesn't matter.It doesn't matter anymore because you're dead. I wear your skin and bone in ashes around my neck and I try to forget the version of you who lived in that room and rotted away. Alive in my head isn't good enough but for the pot roast in her pocketbook Nana and the beat me in Casino Nana and the velour Adidas tracksuit Nana. But being alive for so many versions of yourself means I have so many of you to mourn for and nothing doesn't feel like loss right now, because nothing is ever as it was a moment ago. *Do you think about dying* I asked her, maybe I was 7, awake from a bad dream, clinging to her in the night. *I'm not afraid, dear*, she said. And it comforted me, then. What could I have done to comfort you? Because you told me you were scared right at the end. Even as I watched your heart rate fall and your jaw unclench, your eyes still sought fitfully

across the room for something to make sense of, you grabbing for my wrist,
not remembering the room that you were dying in, and asking for your
mother. Is it just eternal return in its completion? The last breaths we take
are from small, shriveled bodies, we, crying something reptile, begging for
our mothers?

Drink a toast, Nana's dead.
She loved me more than anyone ever could.
They say that a long life is not a tragedy,
That surrounded by your family is not a tragedy,
That living longer than everyone you knew
when you were young is not a tragedy,
but it is.
It's just
quieter.

It's Five O'clock Somewhere

I.

You always know how to manage in a crisis.
Don't think too hard about why that's true.
Pockets full of gauze; an inherited knowledge of medicinal herbs.
You take care of the wounded:
of heart, of mind, of skin's abrasion.
You have come to expect nothing of others.
They will call on you and you will rush to tending.
When you cry out in pain you will hear only the echoing return of your
own voice.
In the woods, be mindful of the snare that knows you are coming.
No one will rescue you, once trapped.
You wish you could become a solitary bear, protective of her spoils.
You don't always need to share your only water.

II.

But, I want to be an albatross.
Not worn around the neck,
so much as free of burden.

III.

I make dinner because that's
what you're supposed to do.
I fill the house with plants.
I walk around the neighborhood and in these hours
of potent reflection reduced to flagellating self-indulgence,
I find all the right songs to rip into my soft sides.
I stay up too late,
ghosts on loop float above me
strung out like garlands.
I am sorry for everything I've ever done
and haven't done yet.

Taking My Vitamins

Eleven supplements a day I'm still
disappearing (shinier hair longer nails
glowing growing gone) the day breaks into
something less recognizable every
painstaking rumination just an excuse for
bad behavior don't do the thing you do
where you blame everyone else for not
making you feel whole-er the proof is in the
porridge all the raisins spell out "mercy"
you're still looking for the golden one.

Taco Tuesday

Because I'm ordering too many soft tacos
for one person to eat alone,
I pretend I'm on the phone with some non-existent lover at
the drive-thru speaker and feign a conversation.
"What did you say you wanted, honey? Three soft tacos?
Sounds great, I'll get a couple for me, too. See you at home!"

But we
(the voice on other side of this speaker & I)
both know there is no Honey.
Any sweetness has completely left my life.

Five soft tacos in a row on a Tuesday.
Eat a taco. He loves me.
Eat a taco. He loves me not.

Should the meaning of life ever reveal itself to be
just a handful of intermittent moments of great revelry,
let it be known that tonight I've finally arrived
to the following conclusion:

Winter and I don't appear to get along very well.

I've started to develop a pattern.
These days, I can't seem to achieve an orgasm without bursting into tears.
I can't decide which is worse: crying in front of a stranger
or getting myself off and doing it alone.

What if I never make love to someone
I care about again and I keep having to fake
intimacy while having real orgasms and then watching
the random man I've decided to take home curl his face in horror
while I sob softly into his junk?

I always want what I can't have and I always want too much.
Sometimes constant conflict is the closest thing to real passion that I have
but I keep spiraling out in the void of it.
How can I be mad at so many people at once?
It couldn't possibly be that everyone else is the asshole, could it?

But April, come she will.
And soon? Nothing left to do but heal.
Somehow, that feels harder.

That's Fine

You don't want me
and I'm supposed to keep feeding myself.
You don't want me
and I have to go to work tomorrow, take on business as usual.
You don't want me and sure we can just be friends!
You don't want me and the dogs still have to shit
and the neighbors still expect me to wave
and the gas man is still coming Tuesday
and every spinning axis is still on its intended course but mine
and I can never touch myself again because you touched me.

You don't want me and I still have to fold my laundry.
And I still need to get sponges and take out the trash.
How am I supposed to just get up from one room
and traipse mindlessly to another
knowing that you are existing right now, quite close by,
in this very moment, going about your business
and I'm over here, thinking about
how you've probably just settled in from work, sitting down after
boiling some tea, putting your feet up on the chair,
the one I used to occupy across from you so easily,
where you rest now without remembering me there,
completely content to not want me at all.

This Morning, Before Work

I put butter on the cornbread
even though there is butter already in the cornbread.
How old was I when I learned to equate decadence with shame?
Someone must have taught me that.

I eat it at the window, the squirrels
in the tree outside collecting black walnuts,
dropping their considerable husks from
great heights, cracking them open on the ground
in the frosty morning.

Later, when I take out the dogs,
I pay special mind to walk atop the shells,
the satisfying crunch beneath my feet feels at least
like a connection to something,
if only the earth below me.

In the trees the squirrels
munch their walnuts joyfully,
chittering and chirping back and forth.

They eat their fill, and then some.

I imagine they do not
feel ashamed.

Compost Pile

You hurt my feelings
and it makes me want to stop recycling.
You don't care about me
so what does it matter
if I let the fruit spoil in the fridge?
You told me.
You told me, if you leave it on the counter
the flies will be relentless,
so I put the bowl of pears and peaches
in the fridge because
I do everything I can to be better than I am
and I forgot them anyway.
What would you think of me,
taking them from the bottom shelf
all molded and ruined,
tossing them right in the compost?
To ripen, and be overlooked, never tasted.
You would say, "What a shame!"
And really, you would be saying what a waste.
What a waste you are.
And I already know all of the bad things
about me, you just say them with a sharper tongue
so they land a little heavier
and all I can think to do is whisper "pathetic"
over and over and over to myself
until I barely even realize that I'm doing it.
Just a song I sing on loop, a daily affirmation.
What a waste.

It's not even a metaphor for anything.
It's just rotten fruit. And an empty bowl.
A disappointed fly looming
over the kitchen island and how
I just need someone to tell me that I'm good,
that a bruised pear is still worth something,
so I don't lose myself completely in this spoil.

Blue

In the persistent ache of winter
there is comfort in cooking
chicken dinners for one.
There is no warm hearth to tend to,
not anymore.
Just me, in the kitchen,
socks sliding along the linoleum,
the cat, nudging my ankle with her chin.

It is not the joyful cooking of company,
though I want it to be more poignant
than it is.
I wear an apron, for nobody.
Listen to Joni Mitchell
like so many sad women before me,
and know that
my sad story is so many sad stories
woven into the collective of ages.

But, it feels good to make something
from scratch.
There are no compromises:
skin on, bone in, butter on my hands
filling each crevice with herbs and oil.

You might say, it's a distraction.
You might say, it's something to do.
Later on, I will joke about how the chicken doesn't judge,
to no one in particular, maybe to the chicken itself.

And I'll wish I had someone else to talk to.

I want to be walked in on,
wiping grease on the tea towels,
sipping the cooking wine, singing to myself
in the oven-heated hallway,

and for whomever it is
who should catch me there

to sigh, and say
"I love you, just like
this."

Blended Family

In my dream,
I tell everyone who's ever hurt my feelings
how much I love them,
and they all leave me on read.

I still feel exactly the same
as when I was seventeen.
I'm waiting for something to move me.
Do people know how boring they are,
with their air fryers and their timeshares?

I wish I could be boring.
I wish I was someone's mother/
I wish I wasn't everyone's mother.

Maybe all it takes is a nice centerpiece
for the dining room table and polished hardwood floors
in a flipped colonial to be fully realized.

Maybe I've been doing it all wrong,
this spelunking into the void of meaning.

Maybe I should buy myself a Vitamix and just give up.

Living Room

Dog-Hearted

I want to be shameless
as my dogs, the way they look forlornly to the door,
in wait for you.

I want to flop down on my belly and cry
all longing and dejection when every car that passes
is not your car, is not your arrival.
To stare, big-eyed out the windows, not understanding
why you do not come anymore to lap up my affections the way
I thought you always would.

"Don't be stupid!" I hear myself barking at them,
when they whine, full of hope should the house stir or settle.
But I pat their soft heads, wishing to take away this dull ache
that we share in our despair. I like to think we are all remembering
the same specific morning, making breakfast and wagging about in our
contented abundance. Blueberry pancakes and Leonard Cohen, right?
But how could they know except to live in the deficit
of their master's sadness, which is a language we all understand together.

I fuss about the apartment and gather armloads of things from
one room to another, the way you are supposed to do, in a busy
and unsorrowful kind of way.
I do not pause for remorse. I do not still to be wistful.
And if I do think of you, it is only for the dogs
who cannot know you're never coming back,
who gaze stolidly at the unmanned door and
rest their paws atop their sweet, soft heads.

"It's over," I try to console them. "Don't be so sentimental."
As for me,
I do not miss you at all.

Pack Animals

The cat and I have sebaceous cysts
at the same time and the big dog
has allergies, and the little dog is
depressed and if the functionality
of your pets is a reflection of your own
existence then we are failing to thrive
and every time I sit around for hours at a time crying
for no reason I want to apologize to them for not being at the park
or teaching them how to be better at tearing meat off a bone
or sniffing out the hunt or being all that very much
useful at anything, really.
But we all sit at the window and watch the snow
and it's almost enough, having them here
in this great big lonely nothing,
and when I lay my head on the big dog's neck,
the little one sighs and the cat lifts her head.

It's almost enough, but nothing ever really is.

Scream Queen

If I were a horror movie girl, I'd be one of the first to go. Stabbed in the back while having sex with the dumb boyfriend character who I wasn't pure enough to reject because I should have been doing my homework. Brain-splattered by the zombie while trying to save some already undead lost cause secondary character who failed to protect me from the onslaught of danger I warned was coming, failed to take me seriously, failed to believe me and then died pitifully on me while I sacrificed my mortal self only to be consumed alive in my own grief. The kind of death the audience will mourn for but say they saw coming all along.

Or maybe I'd just be the woman who chose to walk alone at night, the first victim of the movie to establish the danger to come, not even a speaking line, just screaming myself hoarse and raw, putting up a fight but dying anyway, then, cut to the woman who you're actually meant to care about. The one who climbs out of the near-death experience covered in blood and carnage, victorious and pretty, not a hair out of place, ready to move on and face her trauma head-on and well-coiffed.

What I mean to say is, I'm not a survivor.
I would go up the stairs instead of out of the house.
I would choose the shitty boyfriend, begging him,
"How could you? I thought that you loved me..."
while he's choking the life out of me.
I'd walk the dark alley and not run fast enough
from the stalker with the knife
and should a demon need a soul to snuff out,
I could be that soft landing for possession.
The point is, I don't make it out alive.
The point is, I'm the funny one who takes one for the team.
I'm not the character you root for in the end.
I'm just the foreboding lesson:
you should have turned around.
You should have run downstairs.
You should have locked the door.

Winterized

Grief is an unruly minefield.
I wish you hadn't left your snow boots in the living room.
Also, I found the drawer of pictures that you left.
You either couldn't bear to look at them any longer
so you blindly stuffed them in the bureau,
or you knew that somewhere down the line
I would be mindlessly putting away old clothes
and happen upon them and gasp,
shatter into thousands of raw shards,
the way you must have felt when you shoved them in there.

It is too much to hold sometimes.
How I know that if I called you,
told you to come on home, you would.

I don't want that kind of power.
But sometimes, oh god,
the apartment is so empty and
you are still everywhere in it,
and it's not like I don't think of you.
It's not like I wanted it to end this way.

I think of how your mother must hate me now
and I know that she thought I would save you.
But fucking look at me.
I have always been the disappointing type.
I tried to warn you.

"You don't know how to be happy/
uou don't know what.to do with it."
That's what you said. I don't feel alive if
I'm not at the hand of my own suffering
but once, when things were new and I had so much hope for us,
I watched you cut up the plastic rings from a six pack of beer

and your dedication to the task made me believe in something.
Sea turtles.
And us.

I'm sorry I didn't hold up my end of the bargain.
You know, I was afraid of this.
I recognize myself more in the ache of my own loneliness
than I ever did with someone holding out for me to settle in.

It is too trite, too unabashed,
to tell you that I never meant to hurt you.
I didn't, but that doesn't change anything.
It's just what people say when they don't want to face the anguish
of their own betrayal.

You hurt me, too. But,
that doesn't feel right either.
Just,
I have this secret hope that one day,
if we should happen upon each other at the grocery store
I'll remember the kind of yogurt that you liked with breakfast
and hand it to you nonchalantly,
all is forgiven.
We smile, and walk each other to the parking lot.

In the fantasy, you are happy.
I am still alone.

In the meantime,
I'm not sure what to do with these pictures,
in this drawer, so I turn them face down, and gently
pat their backs and tuck them in.

I'm not even sure if you'd like that,
but it's the least that I could do.

Single Bedroom

Fair Weather

I'm thinking about him in his bright blue underwear
and his mismatched socks, crawling over me into bed,
falling asleep with the movie on and saying
Don't fidget! and me, repeating
fidget fidget fidget,
until it's not a word anymore, and he is snoring,
and I'm just watching him next to me,
in front of the window by my bed, and all the weather.

& we don't talk a lot about serious things
but sometimes he hugs me so hard it hurts my chest,
and I can't tell if he really loves me,
my messy hair and my thunder thighs, my dirty mouth…
or if he just needs someone to love so bad
he'll take waking up next to me,
over waking up alone.

Acts of Service

In the parking lots of his former lives he points out sentimental booby traps to inform me he was once a small-time king in this nothing town. "This is my love language," he says. "Nostalgia." He nods to the movie theatre in the run-down shopping center, where he felt up his best friend's twin sister and found his sea legs in infuriating sexual confidence. He wants to show me everywhere he's been.

He is all I've ever wanted in a prom date, all earnest-eyed and "this song reminds me of you" standing squarely in front of the leering man at the gas station, "I just want to make you feel safe," out loud and unencumbered. Maybe the secret to having the perfect high school boyfriend is waiting 20 years after graduation, and knowing bad habits never die.

I want to give him everything. My love language is slowly dissolving into someone else so I don't have to be with myself anymore. And he will happily devour me. Is trying on new ways to bask in the illicitness of it all. The moment I give in, he'll stop wanting me. He is ripe indiscretion and calculated moral regard: both of us over-analyzing each other's intentions and constantly reminding the other how often we've been hurt before. I love you, he says. If I were actually 16, I'd say, "You shouldn't love girls like me," but it's less cute the closer I get to 40, and honestly, it's nice to hear. We aren't sneaking out of our parent's second story windows. He has crow's feet. I have sciatica. What are we playing at here?

On Halloween, he shows me off at a costume party, says we're dressed up as a real relationship and holds my hand for the first time in public, where nobody knows we're doing something wrong. We should go on tour together, he says, like we don't have jobs or indifferent partners, or lonely dinners to go back home to. We leave early, he drives my car and takes the back roads. There's no poetry in a parkway. We land at a lover's lane and lament how loud the kids are in the next car over and I twinge, thinking they're just doing the same thing we are, but with the wherewithal to actually make out. When they leave, I get out of the car to pick up their abandoned trash and he pulls me back. Don't bother, he says. You can't save the world. But I crouch down in the dirt and collect their abandoned cans and wrappers. I'm only trying to make myself feel better, that's all anything ever is.

I just want a clean fix off an old habit. This is not the first time I've let a man-child make me promises while leaving things a mess at home. If I wasn't a walking worst-case scenario, we would be together. he's a middle-aged Jordan Catalano, and I'm damaged goods Claire Danes—we'd be kissing if I wasn't crying against the dashboard. I want to touch you so bad, he says. Is it better to keep those words in a locket round my neck, or just let go and lose myself in his lap?

My love language is never wanting what I have, so there's no good ending. Just a stretched-out tension in a steamed-up car playing songs to each other that serve as the soundtrack to our wanting. He's so insolent and barefaced, used to getting his way. You know as well as I do, we'll never be just friends. Almost scornful, almost mad. We return to the movie theatre parking lot. He presses his forehead against mine, parts his lips before I turn away, already crying. He leaves me in my passenger seat, staring me down sadly as he drives away in his own car.

I drive home with all the windows open, scream-sobbing into the open air. When I get home, I tiptoe in like a guilty child, I quietly undress facing the wall. Seems to me no matter how this whole thing ends, it won't be good for anyone. I glance at my phone, hide the light under the covers, and read like a sneak in the dark as my unassuming husband softly snores: I miss you already. But it's all tricks of the light and movie theatre parking lots, some wistful, sad story about all that's wasted on the young.

Near Sided

The optometrist's office
is a good place to burst into tears.
If you sob softly enough to yourself,
everyone will just assume you've had
your pupils dilated.

Every age-appropriate thing I've ever tried to do
has ended in irreparable failure.
Not built for marriage. Can't seem to
save any money. Didn't keep the baby alive.
Not to brag, but I'm also insufferable.
Ask anyone.

The receptionist at the check-out desk
hands me a pair of those flimsy sunglasses
before I leave and says,
"These should make things a little easier."

I decide to wear them for the rest of my life.

Making a grocery list a week after seeing you last

Roma tomatoes
Spinach
Goat cheese
Hot peppers

I can't stop thinking about us in that bed that wasn't ours and how you've
ruined any chance of me ever moving on by being so good to me. For
knowing me so well. It must be hard on you, this rising tide, this constant
pull. You can't keep doing this.

Olive oil
Rolled oats
Heavy cream

You were trying to find the kindest way of saying you had your reasons.
For not choosing me. You didn't say if things had been different, but you
shouldn't have said that other thing. When you laced your fingers through
mine, I knew what you meant. But I shouldn't have let you touch me.
Every time I see you, I'm undone. I can't keep doing this.

Fennel
Sunflower seeds
Cucumber
White vinegar

One cocktail too many and I accidentally told you the truth, I think.
Except for how this isn't good for me. If I keep letting you live on the
highest shelf how can anyone else compare? You never told me to wait for
you, you wouldn't do that. But there are certain things you can't take back.
I miss you so much it makes me shake. How long will it take me to right
myself this time around? We can't keep doing this.

Eggs
Honey
Breadcrumbs
Raw meat

The title of this poem is whatever the onomatopoeia is for the sound a dog makes when she's panting

The big dog fell off the bed
and now she thinks she cannot get back up.
I want to explain to her that she
can just jump on as she has always done.
That next time does not guarantee another fall,
but she is big and dumb and sweet
and stands crying at the foot of the bed,
too heavy for me to lift her.
So I cry too, because I can't explain it to her.
Because I don't want to sleep alone,
and neither does she.
If I were smarter, I would know
what sort of metaphor for life this was,
but my dog and I are just sad
in this untranslatable wait for the night to be over,
for her to forget what she couldn't do yesterday.

Cereal, probably

It is more than being overtired, I know,
that I find myself, third night in a row,
toying with the solitude and whimsy of the lost, bent spoon
under the bed, covered in dust, stuck to the floor
perhaps in the ectoplasm of a hundred ghosts
that rocked me to sleep on former evenings,
such as these when the *soul*,
or whatever meaning is,
feels so saturated by a film of loss.

Do not bother to ask me how the spoon got bent,
or what I was eating in bed that time
or even, how a spoon finds itself to be so lost,
as me,
tonight,
beneath the place that cradles me,
will never be the womb again,
and other things that keep me up, awake,
and aching.

He has nice words. You tell him that, and he laughs at you. "Aren't you a writer?" He asks. Half the time you can't tell if he's making fun of you or trying to sleep with you. He wants you around, that much is clear. It has nothing to do with you, of course. You are just the closest thing to care about and you should only be so lucky that he is allowing you into his orbit, which you both know is empty of other planets. Only blown out balls of gas and sunken stars from lightyears before when he was still relevant. He will tell you how much you mean to him but forget everything you say. He's quick with his "I love you" but he's hurtful, and insults you often. He just likes having someone to say it to, but you suspect he'd spit right in your eye given the opportunity. You sit on the edge of his bed and surreptitiously stack his table-side books, fold dirty shirts into a corner on the desk and hate yourself for your woven-in domesticity, the subtle art of taking care. You want, at least, for the sheets to be clean. You have never known such loneliness, between you there is so much sorrow. You don't know where yours ends and his begins. There's nowhere else to go tonight, and he's asked you over. Besides, you've cried yourself to sleep two nights in a row and this, at least, is something different. He likes to see you sad. It makes him feel important. They love you when you're defenseless, when you're pliable, when they can lift your arms from hugging your own chest and find the softest parts of your belly. You suck in your breath, your fear a palpable thing you can touch, and he laughs. You don't matter. You already know. Whatever he does to you will be less painful than the lie you tell yourself, which is, *you deserve better than this*. If that were true, you'd be somewhere else entirely. But you let him use you up and waste your worth and when you are no longer entertaining him, he will find reason enough to slowly disappear and you can say, see? What do I always say? Just like a man. And you will know it is because nobody ever really stays. Not even you.

EN SUITE BATH

Loneliness is a House

The house where you are sleeping is not your house.
You are trying it on; a consignment dress.
Here, you take long soaks in the deep bath,
scented with lavender salts, trying desperately not to see
the reflection of your own body in the faucet.
The wind rattles the storm doors downstairs, a familiar trembling
and you are a child, peeking eyes out from the down quilt
somehow still afraid of the dark.

You make good on your promise to eat at the dining room table,
and to eat well. No crumbs in the bedding, no potato chips
on the couch. You read while you eat yogurt and fruit, like a fraud.

The house is too lovely and unspoiled to own filth,
so you've convinced yourself that every stray speck of dust
or lurking cobweb must belong to you,
you bring the rot wherever you go,
so you crouch small behind the pellet stove
and the couch, to sweep away the ruins with your hands.

You have named the shower spider Laverne.
You bring her offerings, a dead fly from the sink-side
but she'd rather kill her prey herself, and you think that's admirable.
When she waggles a spindly leg about her web, you wave back to her.
Not entirely alone, at least.

You wait for someone to notice that you're missing.
You haven't really gone, but something has been snuffed out.
You are raw and sunken, a widow in a billowy nightgown,
an orphan crying at the top of the stairs.

The punchline is that,
there isn't one.
The house will stand while you wither inside of it.
The windows will rattle but the glass will not break.

You are the poor foundation and the terrible bones.
They will tell you a renovation is useless, and if you're smart,
you'll carry out the demolition.

The Conjuring 5?

Back when things were good between us
we used to come to this theater
to watch scary movies because the
audience participation was always good
and we liked the build-up to the jump scenes.

But tonight, the popcorn is all kernels &
the stoned teenagers in the back of the room
are talking too loudly and
there's a creeping sense of foreboding
(for myself, and everyone else not twitching with sorrow right now)
that has nothing to do with this shitty plot
and every time I turn around and hiss "shush!"
I feel like the embodiment of everything I hate about myself.
Except I've never been the kind of person to shush teenagers
in a movie theater. This part is new. She's bitter and hates fun.

On line at the concession stand, you call me *"Babe"*
& I stiffen. The familiarity of the word
is a jacket that used to fit but never will again.
It just hangs limply, too small,
in the back of the closet and never quite
zips up each time you make a clumsy attempt to pull it closed again.

But you can't donate your failing relationship
to the Goodwill, so I just say,
"Please. Don't."
And the space between us grows wider in our seats.

Back at home,
I cry silently in the bathroom until my face becomes a
warped ghoul in the medicine cabinet.
I brush my teeth until my gums bleed.

In the days before you move out for good,
we will recall how bad the movie was,

but the truth is,
I can't even tell you what we saw.

Skincare Influencer

In the dog days of grief I have developed
something like a near-fixation on my skincare routine.
I don't know what is normal in this new iteration of my life:
Is it just,
approaching 40, to be so concerned with
dark circles under the eyes?
Or will the shadowy orbs dug deep into my bones give way to
black holes that I might fall into
if I'm not more careful? Will I get stuck inside this
vacuum where I just keep discovering
over and over and over
that the baby isn't coming home alive?
I shake it away.
Do not go there. Please. Stay here. Here. Here. Here.
I talk to no one in particular but my reflection,
I pretend the woman in the mirror is just administering
her nighttime tutorial. I listen to her. She seems to know
what she is talking about. I am safe with her.
Everyone over 30 should use a retinoid before bed.
She smiles at me, faced slicked with squalene.
There is something about the ritualized and tactile
motions of applying cremes and gels that keep the flashbacks at bay:
Double cleanse, serums, moisturizer.
Today, I'll use the gua sha just for fun.
Who doesn't love a little lymphatic drainage?
When I rinse my face, I do not hear the
beeping machines, or remember emptying my breastmilk in the sink,
or have to think too hard about how loud it's been inside
the lonely forest of my own undoing.
Don't forget to take breaks with your more abrasive products/
Allow the skin to purge, and the cells to regenerate.
I roll a jade stone over my jawline and the woman in the mirror
pinches the plump apples of her cheeks and says,
This is how you know the Niacinamide is working.

The woman in the mirror knows what Niacinamide does,
but I do not. I want to believe her.
It's something between self-care
and *not* suicide.
Tomorrow is not a Retinol day,
so by default,
I'll have to live 'til Thursday.
Lather, rinse, repeat.

Nursery

Trophy Wife

I.

At the coffee shop, I fantasize about unceremoniously laying out my baggage one suitcase at a time. I would open them proudly, take out my crimes like souvenir trophies and polish them before you, say "this one here is divorce"—blow the particles off a dusty bauble, announce "oh and here's old devoutly mistrustful." I'd line them up next to "failed motherhood" and "adulteress," "disorganized banshee" and "wears too much makeup." You would smile, charmed by my guile, and say "Ahh, 'insolent wino!' I love a gal who knows herself…" and trail off, gazing at me adoringly in total acceptance. The words forming in the back of my throat are shaped like "Run!" and "Escape while you can!" and…something something woman scorned. I don't want to do any more damage. I can't rack up anymore debt. Instead, I let you buy me a cookie, and just tell you what you want to hear. You say, "I'm really excited to get to know you."

II.

I think about how tonight my therapist actually said, "You're never the problem!" and wonder if I've been lying to her outright this whole time and never noticed I was doing it, or if I've honestly just charmed her into believing I'm not a walking pile of trite chaos in sensible shoes.

III.

I bring home my trophies alone and display them on the mantle. I kiss the top of each one like it were a newborn baby's fragile crown and I beam at them, because it's the dignified thing to do, to look upon your sleeping babes and nurse them, nourish them, keep them alive.

Chicken Little

It's almost been a year since the baby died.
I am not well.
I drink wine alone, standing in the kitchen.
I cry into the mirror, looking at the way my face has aged.
I play house with a man who doesn't want me,
to distract me from the horror of my life.
I replace the degradation of grief with a lesser evil
but feel no less lonely in his company
than when he leaves. Sometimes I can't
tell if I'm insatiable with longing,
or if I've always been starving
so I take whatever scraps I can get
and store them in my cheeks.

I've stopped saying yes
when I don't want to. And I want
so little anyway. Or so big,
sometimes I can't tell. I don't know
how to live inside this dying world, that
took my son. How am I supposed to keep
thrumming along to this impossible din? I don't
jump off the ledge, though I edge along
so many cliffs, with such shaky confidence.
I think if my boy were alive, I'd still
be lonely, but I'd be less afraid. Or
more afraid. Sometimes I can't tell,
what is my own heart breaking, or the sky
that is falling and no one believes me when
I say that
I

can't
take
one
more
thing.

Sometimes, I want to scream loud enough
so you would know how much I mean it.

Mostly,
it's easier to say
"Oh. Everything's just fine."

Beat a Dead Horse

Did they blindfold me? Or were my eyes just clamped so tightly shut
and that is why I can't remember their faces?
Did I imagine one of them pressing his
hands over my nose and mouth or could I just
not breathe because I was panicking?
Was the TV on in the living room and was the taller one really laughing?
Did the smoking one say, "Just put it in your mouth?" or did
I hear that in a movie maybe, about someone else's life
and this didn't happen to me at all?
Did one of them sound like Carson Daly or was TRL on while
they held me down and took so much away from me?

I drift off somewhere pleasant. I know enough about being so close to
death that the moment itself doesn't scare me. When an old horse is
dying, she stops pacing in her stall. She lays down heavy, soft whinny,
nostrils flaring. If she's lucky, someone loves her, and is with her
before she goes. Stroking her leathery snout, untangling the last of her
thinning mane. Quietly, gently they whisper into her flicking ear,
"There, there, old girl." I am the mare I am the mare I am the mare.

You can live inside the fear forever
or you can bury it in the mineral earth of your childhood home
and pretend it never happened.
At some point, they must have finished.
They must have stopped smashing my swollen face
against the wicker headboard and let me alone.
I must have gotten dressed again,
and went back down the hall,
waited for my mother to get home
and did my homework,
ate dinner,
showered,
and readied for bed.

Don't.
Don't think about how your sister stood in the corner wearing your clothes
and cheered them on and cackled. Wanted for your hurting.
Keep your eyes closed old girl,
just pace the stall.
It's almost over.
Besides, she will be dead before the memory comes into full focus.
And no one ever
has to know.

Oh please don't wake the baby

Cause there's nothing you can do
Her mamas got it covered
Cause that's what a mama do.
Her daddy done and left her
Couldn't bear to say goodbye
Under the spell of winter
He believed that he would die.
And a woman's always lonely
That's what brings the men around
But the baby cries all morning
And the man don't make a sound.
He's just watching out the window
While his woman feeds the child
She don't know what he's been drinkin'
But he's been drinkin' it a while.
Oh please don't wake the baby
She barely slept all night
She woke up scared and crying
Listening to them fight.
Mama's in the kitchen
Stirring up some jam
And she knows what Daddy's thinkin'
Cause he's only just a man.
There's a lonely road before them
A mother and her girl
Hardened by a sorry lesson
Before springtime wings unfurl.
She's not taken to the breast
and it's kept the child from sleepin'
And her mama's up all night
While her daddy does his creepin'.
Please don't wake the baby

It's no use to stir her now
Her life is changed forever
But she's too young yet to know how.
Oh please don't wake the baby
There's nothing you can do
Her mama's got it covered
cause that's what a mama do.

Such as it Is

I wish autocorrect would stop suggesting the word "pregnant" while I'm going about my menial tasks and replying half-heartedly to my morning business. "I hope this email finds you pregnant." "Let's check in later, tomorrow I might be too pregnant." As though the world is not relentless enough, as though every haphazard step I take forward is not a blind groping scuttle back through a landmine.

There was a mother at the supermarket waiting in the deli line. I watched her boy, no more than one, repeatedly throw the same toy on the ground, reject a bottle, and scream. The woman, dark circles like tree rings under her eyes, looked at me, searching for compassion. "Want a kid?" she asked, exhaling a half-laugh. How do you explain to someone the simultaneous gut-punching relief of uninterrupted shopping and the sudden empathy for desperate women who kidnap babies in grocery stores? No one wants to hear the truth, anyway. I pick up his toy the next time he throws it and walk away without my turkey.

I would have sixteen more c-sections and a dozen more botched epidurals to never be called "brave" again. Mothers are brave, even when their babies live. You only call me brave because there's nothing else to say. I probably wouldn't have been a very good mother, anyway.

BACK PORCH

Like the Cat that Got the Cream

My cat and the weekday mailman have a relationship I have nothing to do with. It is nice, how she makes friends without my intervention—has a life of her own to keep up. Like me, she hisses and bites, protests the attention of too-available men, is haughty and tempestuous and loud. Unlike me, she needs for nothing and desires little. As such, her respect is well-earned and her presence welcomed. Though she rejects the advances of over-eager affection, she loves the mailman and waits for him dolefully on the weekends he has off, celebrates his Monday morning arrival with excited chirps of delight.

From my desk, I peer out the window, and she, sunbathing on the porch, turns belly up to greet him as he approaches. I can imagine the hum of her purring as he kneels to stroke her soft fur, can hear him through the thin glass calling her "Sweet Girl" and cooing to her. He doesn't know I am watching—eavesdropping over their friendship like a greedy troll.

If I were more interesting, my shortcomings would be poetic like my cat's: feral, untamed, gleefully sadistic, woefully irreverent, skeptical of any blind gesture of love. We are alike in some ways, certainly, but even she knows how to let in the softness. My toxic traits are just a list of too much wanting—jealous am I even of the little cat. The word thirsty hangs in the air like a magic coin and though I tuck it behind my ear as often as possible, I know it is the truth.

See, I don't know what it's like to unclench under an open palm and trust it to return without transaction. I am always only witnessing tenderness as an outsider. From this angle it looks so effortless, and then, at once, completely out of reach.

Homesick

Maybe you are cut from the ornate cloths
of all my old-world beliefs,
those delicate parts that cling to spirit guides
and energetic pathways.
Maybe we have enclosed upon each other before in past lives,
when I had healing hands and you were the hunter.

Maybe I am just afraid to settle.
My people are transient,
afraid to dig our feet into the ground,
fear roots, fear growing into one earth for too long.
The soil is not rich enough for vegetation
and I have taken to running from sturdy foundations.

You are fault lines and seismic upheaval.
You would never allow for an overstayed welcome.
Wisdom says we are tempting fate, passion calls you hero
and digs my fingers into your upper crust, says,
"We could be fertile here yet,"

& when you say, "I love you"
I look to my ancestors and beg of them
to untether me from these spoiled crops
and this unsure season that lead me from safety,
into your tillage, where nothing is stable,
least of all the tricks our bodies play on us,
and what it means if the rains don't come and we
don't go to harvest.

Like Breadcrumbs

Regarding your bulk of unprecedented manhood:
Familiar with your lonely trail,
I come lingering towards your salted doorstep
amid the other war-torn survivors of your shoulder-shrug love.
Knowing nothing of your body
but the rate of its lunging,
the rid-me-come-lately's
are beckoned by your beauty,
the promise of your rejection.
Your entropy trail is killing time with tea-bags
and I am but a honey drizzle to your hot-winced swallow.
You cradle me longing and whisper "*Contrary*"—
leave me swollen-eyed ice-skating all the way home.

Rebranding

The sunroom has become the landmark of our avoidance.
Today, after months of stepping over the mess,
we agree to empty it of everything unnecessary.
Cardboard detritus. The old mattress and the litter box the cat hated.
The pictures we chose of each other as children,
we once used as centerpieces.
We put them in a box and taped it over.

It's May.
It's snowing a little.
I want to say something trite about weathering any storm,
but it's not like we did that, so I eat my words and just keep
telling you I'm sorry.
I don't think you'll ever look me in the eye again.

Sometimes, I think I'll open a door
in this house, and enter a completely
different life.

Funny how that happens.

OPEN CONCEPT

"Gift"

At a dive bar in Berlin, a Libyan man buys
me an "American" drink—vodka & soda,
and is relieved to hear that I speak English.

It is February 2020,
and I don't know just how drastically
my life's about to change.

A tall man from the bar follows us out
into the street and punches my companion
in the eye for what appears to be no reason.
Shaken and confused,
I take him to my flat and press a popsicle to his swollen face.

He is embarrassed, but "happy to be here."
Consider it a gift, I tell him.
That shiner will always remind you of the night
that you met me.

In German, he tells me,
the word "gift"
means poison.

If that's not one
giant premonitory red flag
from the universe,
I don't know what is.

But we plant flags into the ground
like seedlings to see what they will become.

We are all colonists of our own demise.

There's a lesson in there somewhere.
But I should have known
and not have offered my tongue
to the dropper so fast.

Viel Glück beim nächsten Mal…

Me: I miss you
Me: I'm right here
Me: No you're not, you're somewhere else.
Me: Where did I go?
Me: To the glazed-over place. You seem to be sleeping.
Me: Well then wake me up.
Me: It's not that simple. You have to want to wake up.
Me: But I do want to wake up. Shake me. Kick me.
        Throw me down or something.
Me: I can't. You have to open your eyes.
Me: But I'm not ready to look around.
Me: Then I guess you're stuck.
Me: I guess I'm the rock.
Me: I guess I'm the hard place.

Babble

Sometimes people talk at me for eleven hours in a row
and then I try to say I'm tired and someone good
says you should be better at telling me you're tired
so I know better next time not to need you
and if you need me you should know how to need me better
and articulate it more eloquently and if you tell me later
then you should have told me before and if you do it one way
then you should do it differently next time and I'll be more prepared
and if all we ever do is talk at each other about being improved
versions of who we currently are maybe in the future we're already
doing it wrong and all this talking in circles is a cover for being scared
and sometimes I'm sure that I'm just Tupperware waiting to be burped
I'm so full of air and I'm so so so afraid of rotting on the shelf

please look at me.

Mikwaukee's Best Dream Boyfriend

I had a dream I was in West Virginia
and I hooked up with this young hick dude
who wanted to take me swimming
in the most dangerous part of the Ohio River and
drink Milwaukee's Best with me in his canoe.

& he lived in this ramshackle house
with his drunk dad and I told him I was 19.
He hit on my sister first, but I just went with it.
"You're prettier than her," he said, and it sounded like
a singing bird.

He was a chef.
He was writing a dissertation.
There was some big flailing fish he caught in the basement.
He might have been lying.
It didn't matter.

Is it a Joke if You're the Only One Laughing?

Bawling in my car on the Lynnway
looking out at the choppy water on New Year's Day.
I want to take the polar plunge
but my body won't let me because
part of it knows that it won't come out and
I'll just let myself drown or even worse, someone
will have to save me, and I'll think of all the other
things I can't do right and it will exhaust me into
compiling another New Year's resolution.
Put that in the bullet journal,
"Drown correctly…"

At a stoplight
the woman in the car next to me
makes meaningful eye contact as I sob unabashedly.
She tilts her head and closely clutches her chest as if to say,
"Oh honey, I know."

I dreamt that all the faucets in the house
had turned the water rust-brown.
Someone I don't know handed me
two small bowls of it and said,
"Maybe try singing?"
I said, "I'm afraid to, because/
what if it isn't true?"
He said, "Do it anyway."

I sang in a voice, much sweeter than my own:
"I am somebody's mother…"
The water went clear,
and we drank it together.

Gratitudes

To Jen, my first reader always, my Wifey, my partner in the microcosmic. Thank you for loving the bugs and the birds, for holding my hand on mountain tops (or even just four-foot slopes), for making room for the mess of my life, and welcoming it in. To Fig, for referring to Ziggy as "Your boy" the way so few people remember to do. And for creating a lovely garden oasis for the sweet, plump rats of Somerville. Thank you both for being the safe place, even when the blankets are cold.

To TJB, VL, IB, WM, KM & JD for the long hospital days and nights, & for holding him for me.

To MP & DC for the grief circles, and immeasurably more than the language of grief has capacity for.

To NC for always using Ziggy's name, knowing about the lilacs, and calling me a "dumb bitch" when it's called for.

To AB, AO, LS, LB, & MM for abetting escape to faraway places, and not forgetting me when I leave.

To Empty Arms, for breathing life back in. To all the other loss parents I have come to know, befriend, and love.

To ML, PMS for lessons and motivations.

To RD & LP for neighborly tidings, and so many saltines.

To AV & UB for nearly everything.

To ASD for making it all better for a little while.

To Game Over Books for seeing a story worth telling in this little collection, and making it real. To Catherine Weiss for knowing exactly what the cover of this book needed to look like, and somehow capturing it perfectly, purely on instinct. Also for the most helpful prompts and redirects, in the absolute most gentlest way, even though I stole those cookies.

To The Bookclub Babes, for the most enduring commitment to literature in the most lovable chaos.

Extra special thanks to Isabelle Correa, Patrick Donnelly, Ian Belknap, and Jendi Reiter for being the first ones to read this collection and spawning the beautiful blurbs on this book that I don't feel deserving of, and yet am endlessly grateful for. These words coming from all of you have not yet ceased to astound me.

Biography

Lauren Singer is a Massachusetts-based therapist and infant loss advocate. She is a staff literary judge at WinningWriters.com and a freelance editor. When she isn't working or writing, Lauren is likely tending to her chaos garden, romping with a dog or two in the woods, in or beside the nearest body of water, or becoming too attached to something (human/animal/inanimate object) and hurting her own feelings. She has self-published five chapbooks, has published work in a wide variety of literary magazines over the last two decades, and is currently working on the completion of her first novel. Raised Ranch is her first full-length poetry collection to be published."